A SEAMLESS BLEND OF ART AND LIFE...

Not a torrential downpour, nor a sudden squall, ***Silence of the Piano Sings*** is fine, steady drizzle that will fairly fantastically make the soil of modern poetry soak up all its droplets.

Teensy-Weensy, Tiddly, Toys or *The Statue of Liberty Falls,* or *I Have Poured My Wine,* or even *Your Eyes Are Orators,* and several divers ideas stock as well as exhibit an exciting range for reader to feast his/her eyes on the symbolically rich images of art the author of this poetic graft has chiseled and finessed.

An avid reader of Time—a period of history, events, experiences of human lives, the world—the poet with his craft and subjective touch weaves webs of fancy around his own experiences before planting them in the soil of Time. He sounds to have taken inspiration from a variety of sources—nature, humanity, realism, art, beauty etc—to fill the canvas of his verse with the paint of an inner psychological struggle; and, very significantly, he styles them on a universal look for reader to identify with his (poet's) characters (his poems).

A Bachelor of Arts in Sociology, Master of Science in Management, and Master of Art in English Literature, visiting lecturer, member of University of Surrey Alumni, member of Chevening Alumni, civil servant, literary and social critic, writer, poet, author of *Sada Syre'a Seer Mein* (a poetry book) **M. Syre** can be visited at www.msyre.com and contacted through email: msyre@ymail.com.

Aamir Latif Siddiqui

Silence Of The Piano Sings

(Poetry)

M. Syre

AuthorHouse™ UK Ltd.
500 Avebury Boulevard
Central Milton Keynes, MK9 2BE
www.authorhouse.co.uk
Phone: 08001974150

First published by AuthorHouse 3/15/2011.

ISBN: 978-1-4567-7385-4 (sc)

Music, when soft voices die,

Vibrates in the memory—

Odors, when sweet violets sicken,

Live within the sense they quicken.

Rose leaves, when the rose is dead,

Are heaped for the beloved's bed;

And so thy thoughts, when thou art gone,

Love itself shall slumber on.

P.B. Shelley

drop by drop

falls

the venom

of

memory!

M. Syre

Dedication:

I dedicate this book to two pearls of my life,

Shumel & ***Aliza*** and my other half, ***Hira***.

Contents

Acknowledgement xv

Preface 1

On Cloud of Drifting Time 13

I Have Poured My Wine 14

I Keep on Taking Puffs at My Life 15

The Bell Chimes 16

I Saw the Silvery Voice 17

The Corpse of My Feelings 20

The Stage is Embellished 21

Touch not Piano Keys, Madame 22

In Thin, Strained, Coughing, Low Voice 24

Your Eyes are Orators 26

What You Sculpt, I Do Not 28

Your Leaning Leans me, Pisa 29

The Ice Age 30

At a Foot's Distance, Louvre 31

In A Venetian Market 32

Tears in Her Sapphire Eyes 33

Empty like a Trumpet, World 34

Like Attractive Freckles, Paris 35

The Ink of My Soul 37

My Mind's Both Fag an' Fire 38

Cannot Resist the Mind 39

Reality—an Illusion 40

From the Womb of Beaming Bath 41

The Statue of Liberty Now 42

At the Southampton Shore 43
Under The Scorching Sun 44
With One Leg Chopped Off 45
Dancing Wildly Her Swift Body 46
Teensy-Weensy, Tiddly Toys 47
Meanings 48
The Goddess of Justice 49
A Lonely, Forlorn Hill 50
A Blank Canvas 51
He Flings a Framed Mirror 52
The Shepherd Unheard 53
Shifty, Venal, Harlot Minds 55
Oh, Majestic Avon! 56
Not Flabbergasted, Rocked 58
Dreams Hopes Burn 60
A Torso of a Mind 62
Hemlock 63
The Drama 64
At Twilight—I 66
At Twilight—II 68
The Trumpets Blow 70
Birth 71
Thirst, Thirst, Thirst, Eternal Thirst 72
Scavengers 73
Bruno is Burnt at the Stake 74
Catch Tropical Winds 75
Time Melts 77
In the Venetian Water 78

Every Face	79
Insensate Violin	80
Sing to Me no More, Sirens!	81
A Sea	82
Alabaster Statue	83
The Dotted Line	84
The Painting	85
Put Out the Sun	86

ACKNOWLEDGEMENT

I would like to acknowledge the contribution of following souls to the completion of my book:

My Family—sacrificed their due share of space and time to help me get through this book. Thanks for your love and care!

Anna Mendelssohn, Amjad Islam Amjad, Aleja Bennett, Zahid Ali Jatoi, Anthony Watkins and Jason Robinson—offered comments on my poetry. Thanks!

Paul and Fran—a cosmopolitan, complex-free, caring, considerate, loving, perfect couple, who fairly affectionately introduced me to the socio-cultural norms and values of England, which helped me revisit English literature, including this poetic work, in a different way. I owe a debt of gratitude to them.

Contribution of *Friends' International, Rebecca Griffin, Hugh Griffin* and *Jacob*—an old man from the south of Snowdonia Mountains—must not go unacknowledged. The former was a fabulous organization, organized and led in practical terms by Rebecca, jointly with Hugh, who was more of an ardent supporter from behind the scenes. I owe much of my excursion trips especially to Isle of Wight, Cranleigh Village and Send Evangelical Church, to this organization and these persons; reader can feel the influence of these places in my poems as well as the preface; while Jacob who met me at Cardiff gave me the idea of visiting St. Fagan's museum. This museum has much to pay me in my writing, especially this book. A lot of thanks to you all!

Four friends (two of them like Galatea to me)—*Carine Bazine* (France), *Yasaman* (Iran), *Claire* (England) *and Sophia* (Greece)—deserve special thanks for being direct inspiration for some of my poems in this book.

Irene, Reaten and *Manoj Chumble:* Irene (China), for accompanying me to a number of places in the UK and caring all the way about my stay in China and showing me Tianjin, Beijing and Xian; Reaten (China), for being my English guide in Tianjin and Badaling (Wall of China); and Manoj (India), for being with me throughout my stay in the UK and China. These places are one or the other way found reflected in some of my poems. Thanks a lot, guys!

Aamir Latif Siddiqui, Maqsood Mahesar, Agha Samiullah and Abdul Ghaffar Lakhiar for being with me throughout the process.

Asim Rehman Shaikh, for his pleasant company in London, where like Virgil he guided me through the streets of Central London giving description of the minutiae of its history; and especially for his continued support right up to the hilt in getting this book published from Author House Publishers in London.

Last but not least, *Zahid*. Yes, Zahid, I need to thank you, for it was you who always remained there to support me in viewing, reviewing and analyzing the contents, organization and structure of the book from poem to poem including the preface.

M. Syre

From the Thames to Land's End

(Preface)

The Houses of Parliament abut on the river bank as a regal order for the waves to sing tunes of harmony and peace; London Bridge, along with Tower and Westminster Bridges, spreads as a net for winds of people to blow across the space of time; nothing that flies in the mind of the city escapes the amazingly blinking London Eye; the tube stations, towers, high streets, buildings and parks, all alight with passion are justifying their existence. With a glass brimful of red wine, in an open air restaurant on the bank of the river Thames, relishing the presence of the surroundings, I am puffing at my cigarette.

In a long, thick overcoat, Albert Camus moves past my table, a half-smoked cigarette dangling from his lips. Having invited him, I offer him a chair. Flicking the ash off his cigarette onto the floor, he settles himself comfortably in the chair, and looks at me wearing silence on his lips. To break the ice I ask him as to how he feels about London! He gazes intently into my eyes, quotes T.S. Eliot, 'the unreal city'. Puffing furiously at his cigarette, he ignores the ash falling on the floor. I look into his deep eyes and find him lost in *The Plague* and *The Wrong Side and the Right Side*. Each puff he takes at his cigarette prints an image on his face of *Outsider*. So I ask him to accompany me to Paris. He agrees. I take him to *Arc de Triomphe* and *Place des Vosges* to show him how victorious he has been having painted his mind on the canvas of history. Looking around both the sites one by one in a fairly dispassionate way he signifies his disinterestedness. Nonetheless, I take him to the Seine River to take a *Bateau-Mouche Cruise*. In this glass enclosed boat plying along the Seine, we make a tour into the womb of Paris. I still see the same image of *Outsider* emerging out of the plumes of smoke. The cruising finishes and he bids me farewell. While I grope for words, he disappears in the thick of the city leaving behind him rings of smoke hanging in the air. I am left completely immersed in the idea of *Estrangement* Camus reflected through his mood and gestures.

Engrossed in the chain of thoughts, I come to sense the cigarette has smouldered to an end when the fag end drops onto the floor having singed my fingers. Before I settle back, a voice compels my attention. I turn around and see Baudelaire. Full of enthusiasm, he invites me along to the Louvre museum, "Let's rush! There's a grand party of the world's great names. Hurry, lest we should miss it!" I brighten up and betake myself to the museum with him. We enter the museum's grand foyer that radiates an aura of grandeur. I get mesmerized seeing Shelley talking to Aeschylus on their *Prometheus* plays; Goethe opening his collected work of poems for Latif—the bard of Bhit—to flick through its pages; Descartes discussing his *Cogito ergo sum* (I think therefore I am) statement with Kierkegaard; Thackeray, Virginia Woolf and Sophocles trying to comprehend what Freud elaborates about his *id, ego, superego* and *Oedipus Complex*; Machiavelli opening his *The Prince* and reading its introductory lines to Gandhi, and Bacon flipping through the pages of voluminous *War and Peace.* On a corner some of the Romantic maestros are absorbed in description of the harp Euterpe—the Muse of music— has invented; at a side Rodin is requesting Balzac to pose in a straight fashion to carve his full length image; Van Gogh and Raphael are deliberating on the use of yellow on Aphrodite's painting, while Carlyle and Byron are lost in a heated discussion on the concept of Heroes. Besides, many known and unknown figures are seen chatting, discussing, smiling and laughing throughout the foyer. Baudelaire and I meet all of them one by one. Having had the meeting Baudelaire flops down into a chair. I go to Picasso— busy trying to paint Cleopatra, his hand shivering, as the bird of his imagination is unable to unfurl its wings. The giant of creativity lives and dies again and again for its permanent existence, thereby blowing out and lightening the candle of his passion with an uneven pace. Cleopatra smiles at him, obscured. Out of love she appears in her real stature inspiring the bird of his imagination to return to its nest utterly confident to make the artist fill the canvas with the true spirit of the vivacious lady. Letting him enjoy his creative passion, I go back to Baudelaire and sink into a chair by him. In a little while, Mona Lisa breezes into the foyer in her artistic apparel. She sits between Baudelaire and me breathing freshness into our souls. Baudelaire begins to recite his verses to her while I keep extracting verses from her face. The more I look into her eyes, the more the Muse of poetry recites me verses of un-aging love and unending passion. Baudelaire keeps on reciting his verses and she listens to him with unusual fervour. Letting the noted figures present in the foyer rejoice in the party, and Baudelaire and Mona Lisa delve into the realms of beauty and verse, I depart to the Thames.

The Thames flows effortlessly as though it is under the hypnosis of Shakespeare's sonnets and plays. Flowing along its waves, I leave for Shakespeare's birth place, Stratford-upon-Avon—the town that weaves a spell over the ocean of literature. I see the globe paying homage to the great bard. This small town, with its narrow streets brimming with visitors, emanates an aura of dreamlike environment. The verdant landscape of the town is reflective of the fertility the Bard's soul has sketched on the map of literature. I knock at the gates of the Avon. The burbling waves invite me into their veins. The journey begins with my meeting Hamlet sitting with Ophelia in a canoe drifting along the river. They are followed in a boat by Othello and Desdemona, so interestingly lost in each other, that nothing in the environs of the waves diverts their attention. Lady Macbeth on the bank of the river with a dagger in her hands utters repeatedly, "It (life) is a tale told by an idiot, full of sound and fury, signifying nothing". A canoe carries Shylock—hawking his liver around, but is heeded not. A colourful dramatic world appears to rule the Avon. The author of these unparalleled, unsurpassed characters, who have enlivened this magnetizing theatre world, appears in a stately fashion, shakes hand with me, and asks me round for company. We leave for his home where original folios of his dramas and different texts of his poems welcome me. Tragedies, comedies, poems, words, language, heroic passion, feminine courage, characterization, all regaling me with their stories spatter on the soil of my heart as seeds of art. Like two musketeers, the Bard and I shoot at the chains of tradition in literature, which cage the bird of imagination. At the burst of fire, fairies appear with a team of supernatural characters of the Bard's plays to mark the spirit of enlightenment. Undoing Aristotle's unities, princes, princesses, soldiers, commanders, messengers, and others flock to impress on time the significance of liberty in thought. Cleopatra and Juliet dance in the chamber of romance, while Anthony and Romeo hum the tune of love on the harp of Shakespearean lines. This theatre feast engages the evening fancifully. Having this feast of imagination enjoyed, I turn to the Avon saying goodbye to the great Bard.

The river water with its mellow waves carries me to Bath. Jane Austen, with her beaming eyes, welcomes me. We hug each other; I give her a *la bise*. She plants a kiss squarely on the palms of my hands and takes me to Sulis' realm where hot springs breathe history out. Pride and Prejudice, Persuasion, Sense and Sensibility, Mansfield Park, Emma and Northanger Abbey spread on the fertile landscape of Bath as corns of simplicity, care and love. Fragrance and colours of flowers wafting through these fields sketch the map of dignity Bath has been bestowed on. Jane pastes the fragrance and colours of these flowers into my soul while I sprinkle on the soil of her heart the chords of feelings my poems strike with. She opens the pages of her *Juvenilia* to read me the moments she has taken pains in to print her heart on the leaves of time. I pluck the thorns stitched to the cuffs of the pages and fling them to the regions of obscurity. Letting Jane rejoice in flowers of her *Juvenilia*, Bath gleam with Jane's timeless novels, and having affixed my signatures on the waters of Avon, I move back to the Thames.

I am back to the restaurant now. The London Eye crossing the Thames comes near me. I offer her to sit in a chair in front of me; she collapses into it, and uncurls her wavy eyelids to drown me into her eyes. There—in her eyes—I find the Goddess of Justice seated on the throne of Queen Victoria placed at the Osborne House, East Cowes. Sitting by the Goddess, Princess Beatrice recites cantos from *The Divine Comedy*. The Goddess orders *The Inferno* gates to open for the masses to exit and gain their first admittance into *The Paradiso*. The people from *The Purgatorio* instantly run to shoulder the Statue of Liberty about to fall onto the earth. Some of them rush towards the scavengers near the Statue of Liberty to launch an assault on them. Sirens, singing songs of lust and carnal desires, wait in the waters of the Atlantic near the Needles on the shore of Isle of Wight, but the people sail to the west coast of the Atlantic where Virgil waits to guide them to their destination. I take a long pull on my cigarette and blow the smoke out into the eyes of the London Eye. In a wink she vanishes. I speak to her, "Your eyes are orators!"

I knock back my wine and follow my feet to Greece. The route is long, with hills, streams, thorns, zigzag tracks, deserts, plains and meadows. Here I meet the nine Muses waltzing with gods across Zeus' chamber over the Mount Olympus; Menelaus instigating Agamemnon to launch an attack on Troy to get him his sultry Helen back; Lycurgus busy revisiting the world's first constitution he has framed for the Spartan citizens; Heraclitus busy in his philosophy of *flux and fire*; Euripides writing his tragedies; Aristophanes into his comedies; Aeschylus lost in his words, "Against one's will comes wisdom." Ardent followers of Dionysian faith are busy dancing and drinking innumerable bouts of wine flowing from the top of a hill where Dionysus sits with utter charisma. Everyone carouses; everyone is drunk. Streams of wine wave over wave flow freely. Dionysian faith is at its zenith. From the cup of Dionysus wine some Elysian scent wafts to make everyone fall into a trance. Out and out divine, Dionysus descends from the hill having found me standing amidst his worshippers. People draw aside to make space for the god. Wind is muffled, voices are curbed; everyone is surprised to see the god decanting into my glass the ethereal wine! I take the wine glass, bid farewell to the surprised Greeks, and move to Athens.

Crossing the world of Utopia Plato ideated, I reach the point in time when no one in the Athenian streets is found questioning their wit and wisdom, no one is heard speaking on the philosophy of beauty and life, and no one is seen stinging the mental horses of Athens as a 'gadfly'. Times are haunted by bleakness of its kind. At a fair distance from this time I discern a graveyard. My feet start moving to its direction only to reach there within a short while. The graveyard gives a desolate, forlorn look with its soil crinkled like a dried page in an untouched book. Most of the graves I see are decrepit with stones and bricks crumbling away. I see trees with thick trunks, long curved boughs without a single leaf hanging. My eyes lead me to the grave Socrates is buried in. I tread the path to the grave. Having reached there, I move round it to eventually find its tombstone. The tombstone reads, "*Hic jacet* Hemlock"!

Again back to the Thames, for over several minutes I see London and Westminster Bridges shooting the breeze. I cherish seeing them in a light mood. Cicero barges in on me bringing Anthony round. He has brought something in his pouch to show me, but before doing so, he starts chattering excitedly to himself only to talk to me a little later, while Anthony with a flat face stands aside mute like a picture. I wonder why such a great orator, as Shakespeare has fashioned him into, has trailed off into a sullen silence! At last Cicero unzips his pouch and unfolds a painting of Caesar being stabbed by Brutus and his friends. He wants to plead Brutus' case. I warn him, "See, Oh master of Italian, overtones of feelings, morality or cultural norms are not enough for pleading a case, especially a murder case. Facts are essential to a case as are legal and rational interpretations." Having heard so, Cicero puts the painting on the floor and sits aside silently. Here I see Brutus emerging out of the painting. He bursts, "I know one thing: ambition is the worst enemy of man; and when this enemy seizes the chair of a ruler, it can turn perilous to the state as a whole. It is, thus, for the prosperity of the state and its people this enemy should be taken to task and stabbed to death for a greater good." Caesar follows suit, comes out of the painting and says, "I know Brutus will never climb down. But the question is: why on earth Brutus thinks his friend should be slain? Only to provide him with an opportunity to rule the Romans? Besides, who is going to reap the benefit of my slaughter—the subjects or the murderer? Of course, the murderer! Whatever the situation, the Romans reject the idea of Caesar's killing." I ask Anthony to speak his version to the world, but he acts dumb. Caesar turns angry at Anthony, dresses him down for subsiding into such an icy silence and goes back into the painting, disgruntled. Brutus, with no point to make, follows him. Anthony disappears beyond London Bridge. Cicero drifting along the waves of the Thames vanishes like a dewdrop. Here comes Mozart holding a violin in his hands. He says to me, "Do you see this violin in my hands? This is totally insensate, numb. It does not feel pain when I strike its strings. It knows not who suffer and who enjoy the tunes it frees. It however vibrates to justify its existence that Anthony does not". Utterly sensitive, he seems to be bursting with emotions to talk on Anthony's expected role. I facilitate him to wear his heart on his sleeves. He speaks while I listen. The discussion journeys on a long route till we need to relax a bit; so, I replenish my wine glass and light a cigarette. Getting an affirmative nod from me, he starts fiddling the violin strings belting out rich tunes, which like arrows piercing through the clouds return with drizzling, then rain. The tunes along with the rain dashing against the face of the city echo even after Mozart has left.

Amid the raindrops pelting down on me, I set out for the Tower of Pisa. The moment I reach there, I hear her welcome me, "This is the soil of art. It bristles with episodes of history, which have punctuated Time with snatches of beauty to be eulogized as a diadem on the head of Time. Come and feast your eyes on the lips of art and the face of history." I respond with an engaging smile. With a light tripping rhythm on a melody of bricks holding her stature, she makes me twirl her around. Her twirling and my stepping convert into a salsa dance. Amidst the rain lashing down onto the soil, we trip off along the road of art cleaving the landscape of history. Salsa turns into Beatrice, who makes us take a short tour of the *Paradiso*. It is the *Paradiso* of art where beauty rules, fragrance sings, colours dance, minds fly and hearts smile. We return to Pisa, our minds swinging. The trip is terrifically enthralling, so is salsa. But we have to separate as the Wall of China awaits my arrival.

Beijing at Badaling welcomes me. In the arms of a biting chill crawling on and above the snow-clad landscape on either side, I, like a bird, alight on the Wall of China, exhilarated. In winter clothes, tourists in their multitudes sauntering up and down blanket the Wall as if a long, colourful snake cuts through the white bed of Antarctica. The Wall rings with *Sheeshiye* and *Bookachiye*. Only a fraction of non-Chinese tourists is visible amidst the multitude. In this bustling environment, I find Michael Angelo beavering away at a statue. I knock at his mind, "Hello, great Angelo!" He responds accordingly. "Hey man" I ask, "*Galleria Dell' Accademia* museum craves for you as *Awakening Captive, Atlas, Youthful Captive, Bearded Captive* and *St. Mathew* find themselves unfinished without you, while the statue of *David* pines for you. The frescoes you left indelibly in *the Sistine Chapel* and *the Medici Chapels* are bearing out to the world the exquisite craftsmanship your hands shine with. Why on earth have you selected China for your new carvings?" For a while he smiles wistfully, and replies, "A real artist is a bird that can perch on any bough of Time he feels pleasure in. From the Forbidden City to the Statue of Liberty, I find my destination in the heavens of *Terra Cotta Warriors* of Xian my soul feels flying in." I respond, "Yep, chisel of a real artist carves better in Time than stone." He smiles before immersing himself in dusting of the statue. I add, "How scary and terrifying this statue of a wolf looks!" He draws aside from the statue and looking at it says, "This is" he pauses for a while "death I have been carving in here. Its face does scare off man; its presence, however, is shrugged off. It has many faces; I have sculpted just one." "Yes my friend" we get surprised to see Will Durant, from a little distance treading along the Wall towards us, cutting in on our conversation "let me plunge into the exploration of death you have carved into a new face. I shall be painting some subtle nuances of its picture on the pages of history." Having welcomed him we carry on with our chat. He goes on, "You know? Friends! I replenish the ink of my pen from clouds; because it is attained by those with skills to clamber up the clouds, and especially because this ink is like water: colourless and spineless." Durant looks at Angelo's statue and says, "I see the wolf statue by Angelo fully coloured. But this is the colour my eyes see. When *I* add it to the world history, its colour will vanish." Angelo says, "First of all I have an objection on the term 'coloured'; secondly, reality hinges on interpretations. Death or colours, thus, themselves in a way are interpretations; what is subjective or objective warrants a careful scrutiny; it's not so simple, dear." I cut in, "Let's not plunge into any philosophical discourse, folks." Durant says, "But first I have to answer him." So stresses Angelo. They disagree significantly to each other's opinions and interpretations. The parley pivots on subjectivity, objectivity, death, reality, art and history; however, turns out to be inconclusive. Durant returns to where he had emerged from; Angelo sticks at dusting his statue; I leave for Wales to see Dylan Thomas.

I reach the St. Fagan's museum, an exceptional repository affording the world rich history of Celtic cultural houses. I succeed in finding Dylan blowing a trumpet in his house. Having offered me a chair I settle myself in he asks me to watch around the room especially a torso on a plinth in a corner. I am stirred by the craft the torso is modeled with. He says, "That torso I feel is a torso of mind majority of us on our heads keeps moving with. On that corner you can see a pen and ink with a diary I used to compose my poetry in. I have ditched my writing, for it is not for torsos of mind. I feel alienated having used my ink as it spreads on the pages like anything turning them shriveled. No one can read." "Whatever you contend Dylan, your work cannot be ditched by Time. Like others I still remember your poems." "Do you, dude?" "Yes, certainly; and I can recite if you like!" "Great! Can you recite to me *Under Milk Wood*?" I nod my head in agreement. He basks in his poem I recite to him. Having listened to the poem he says, "Of course, nothing makes an artist downright choked up. The trumpet I am holding is a great medium for blowing my tunes through but there is no ear to hear it and if there is one that turns out to be, indeed not everyone, like this torso." Meanwhile, Wordsworth and Byron enter the room talking to each other on a book titled *Bruno is Burnt*. We attend to them. Dylan, "What's up bards? What's this book about?" Wordsworth, "Hiya, Dylan, Syre, to be brief, it is Bruno's story, the scientist, who was burned at the stake after he had made his theory about the Universe public, which was notoriously repaid with a gift of death sentence. I think it suffices?" He waits for a moment reading our faces and says, "Or we can discuss it later on! At the moment let me fill you in: on our way from Tintern Abbey we found Beethoven crying?" "Beethoven? Crying? Don't tell me! I believe he is stout enough to make others cry!" Dylan rejoins. Byron cuts in, "Not kidding, you know he is hearing-impaired; this is what makes him cry." "Let me add a little detail" Wordsworth continues, "In fact, he was roaming around the countryside with a friend. A flautist played a flute at some strolling distance. Forgetting the maestro's plight, his friend tapped on his shoulder to show him how superbly the flautist played the flute. The moment the maestro viewed the flautist playing, he burst into tears. What a tragedy!" "True" Dylan comes out with a strange note "some cry for not being able to sing; others cry for why they are singing. What a tragedy!" Byron says, "Nothing outside us burns us more than the mind's cosmos persisting within. Once in Venice an Italian shopkeeper in a rude way asked me not to speak to her in English but Italian if I wanted to buy something. For quite a while it discomforted me; but now I feel she might be right in saying so." "I feel" says Dylan "it is only after death we measure men. How many great men have remained consigned to oblivion till they tasted the cup of death?" "No, I disagree" says Wordsworth "I agree to Byron's point: this is the state of mind, whatever the objective reality?" "Ok folks; let's pick up the confab after a break, as I wish to offer you some red wine before serving you special Celt food." We sit together for long sharing our views on Beethoven, life and nature, our wine glasses chinking. Having enjoyed Dylan's company, we depart: Wordsworth to Cockermouth, Byron to London, and I myself to Land's End.

I am standing at Land's End. Everything off the sea seems fallen into a deep slumber; everything towards the sea is increasingly vigorous. Numerous ships in zigzag lines are bidding goodbye to the coast; their echo faintly audible, their shape hazy in the distance. The moonlit waves in the sea seem like the heartbeats life is running under the water with. The surrounding serenity adds beauty to the coastal marvel. I put my wine glass aside stubbing out the cigarette on a stone, and take my violin feeling if I touch its strings they would bleed and cry. But I know if they don't bleed and cry; there won't be music. Hundreds of thousands of songs are drifting on these strings waiting for my touch. I start fiddling the strings with a softer touch; the environment gets blissed out. Seeing the tunes wanting in vibrancy I fiddle the violin with sheer vitality. Music blares out! Tunes spread across the coast to the ships navigating towards the farthest ends.

(This 'preface' is an experiment, as I have not availed myself of the prevailing styles of prefaces coming from *Lyrical Ballads* and even before it. I have, however, tried to make use of fiction to meet my purpose fine. I believe use of fictional or even semi-fictional style, especially for prefaces or introductions to books, can provide both reader and critic with a different flavour. I lay this poetic graft open before the world for critical judgment.

As to my poems, they have, excluding the prose poems, a little variety of metres; main focus on the syllable count; music prevailing over paintings, paintings over statues; stories on the wings of the bird of imagination; the bird of imagination on the bough of a tree rooted in the fertile earth; words suited to contexts, the contexts fitted to ideas, the ideas adjusted to Time, and the Time geared to the soul in order to absorb its shades, hues, colours.)

(Drafted at the Chancellor's Bar,

University of Surrey, England, by the end of 2008;

Finished at Tianjin, China, by February, 2010)

M. Syre

msyre@ymail.com

www.msyre.com

On Cloud of Drifting Time

On cloud of drifting time
Again a Socrates

Holds a cup brimful of
New, raw, lethal hemlock!

Everything's mute an' still!
Everyone's spineless, dazed!

And lo, the cup trembles,
As the venom trembles!

Athens, 2008

I Have Poured My Wine

I have poured my wine
Over Time an' Space.
Everyone is drunk;
Everything is drunk;
Everyone totters;
Everything totters:

Mozart's tunes echo
Through marble arches
Of the Taj Mahal!
Lo, Catullus strikes
Strings of Dun'booro,
Which sway to Bach's grand,
Rare musical notes!
With Kalidasa's
Solemn brush, Van Gogh
Paints Shakuntal on
Red lips of Lesbos,
Where Sappho's verses
Shine with homely hues!
Using Angelo's
Stylish, vital tools,
Sartre cuts the Time
Into the grave hand
Of Samuel Becket!
Shelley's poems, all
Turned a million grapes,
Swing from Homer's vine;
Greece sways back and forth!
Shrines an' forts carol,
Temples just carouse,
Churches sing, while reel
Colonnades of Rome;
Tall skyscrapers faint,
While hamlets bulge with
One deep, strong, chilled draught!

Rome, 2008

I Keep on Taking Puffs at My Life

I keep on taking puffs at my life:
the smoke hangs round me,
everywhere.

utterly wreathed in smoke,
I see the world through it.
at times, the smoke

gets so thick and dense,
I fail to make out anything
across it.

as I puff at my life,
it smoulders to the fag end,
ash sinking into

the ashtray of Time;
the ash strews the tray,
which keeps it

in her bosom
as the Ganges river
keeps the ashes

of a cremated body.
the smoke round me
and the ash

in the ashtray of Time
are my signs, my symbols,
my words, my poems.

the more I puff at my life,
the more the ashtray
welcomes the ash!

London, 2008

The Bell Chimes

sizzling rays
of the solar disc
strike the earth as burns;
the bird of silence flies,
while a gravedigger
gashes its wings
with the blade of his spade.
    the bell chimes:
    hands shiver
    but carry on digging!

the grave has been dug
and the mourners have
gathered around it.
the earth
opens its mouth
to gulp its morsel:
    the bell chimes:
    no one hears,
    save the gravedigger!

with the brush of its
dark, cracked lips,
the night kisses the earth;
the skin of the earth turns wrinkled.
the mourners gather again
in the cemetery,
but this time
the gravedigger
is turning
a morsel himself.
    the bird of silence
    flaps its wings again...

    the bell chimes...

London, 2007

I Saw the Silvery Voice

I saw the silvery
Voice of birds and insects,
Heard the bright colours of

Pristine, untouched flowers!
The stars before me like
Beggars knelt for only

One carefree, lovely glimpse!
Played hide and seek the Moon
Behind the screens of clouds!

I heard wee stones chatter
Inside the veins of hills;
I heard the oceans hum,

I saw the sun smile, laugh,
I walked on wilder winds,
I strolled through galaxies!

I ran through the skies as
An endless cloud of love!
I crept on Mars to see

The earth in ecstasy!
I'd see an old woman
In dinghy of the Moon

Knit one soft mink for me!
I rode on horses of
Warm, starlit, restful nights!

I slept on sea breezes,
I sang in pouring clouds,
I danced in twisters, storms!

O flinty, fiendish Time!
You have frosted my voice,
My catchy, lively songs,

Frozen my melodies
Which flew in rapture like
The songs of kind cuckoos!

You have faded the hues,
Colours which pervaded
The Himalayan peaks,

The valleys in the Alps,
Which I would sip with eyes!
You've stifled the burbling

Of smooth, mellow water
That lapped against the boat
Of my harmonic life!

Now, no more tulips sing,
Now, no more fragrance tells
A tale of gleeful hearts;

Now sketch colours no more
The map of pure romance;
Caged like a skylark my

Transformed soul blubs, wails, cries,
Whose eyes only can kiss
The shining Moon above,

Whose body can kiss tough,
Hard, stiff bars of the cage!
I float with rollers to

The Isles crammed with spears of
A brooding existence!
There was a time when eyes

Could hear an' ears could see!
Oh, Time, oh, friendly foe!
Uncoil the coiling wit

Or open a chink in
Its thick, heavy curtains!
Let my young soul breathe in

Raw, fragrant, fresh, pure air,
Where Keats can sing with me,
Byron can dance with me!

Kashmir, 2005

The Corpse of My Feelings

The corpse of my feelings
Hangs over one bough of

A gnarled, hollow oak tree.
In flocks vultures swoop down

Over the corpse, gnaw it
So wildly that scores of

Pieces of its flesh fall
Onto the ground, where wait

Hyenas in a pack.
Wolves round this tree wait for

These creatures to withdraw
From this banquet. The feast's

Over; everywhere spread
Are the carcass remains.

The night wears on; the sky's
Heavily overcast.

The rain keeps pouring down
Through the fierce, ghastly night.

Now it's day; all is light;
Everything's spotless, clean.

The corpse remains can be
Seen no more on the ground.

Karachi, 2009

The Stage is Embellished

The stage is embellished
With multi-coloured flowers

Glinting in blinding lights.
A full length, oil portrait

Of a grim-faced old man
Adorns the wall onstage

Whereon sit reputed
Orators and critics

To pay tribute to a
Gifted bard of the time.

With each speaker, the hall
Echoes with loud applause.

Books with eyes wide open
On a nest of tables

Beam at the poet, who
Reciprocates the same.

Eyes tear-filled with load of
Misfortune, anguish, woe,

He leaves the hall back to
Badly waiting graveyard!

Hyderabad, 2006

Touch not Piano Keys, Madame

Touch not piano keys, Madame,
Silence of the piano sings!
Let the tunes in piano sing,
Let the piano sing in tunes!
Let the tunes in piano dance,
Let the piano dance in tunes!

I see the world singing and
Dancing through centuries in
These black, white keys of piano!
Touch not piano keys, Madame!

I see nubile, hot Helen
Uncurling her wavy curls
On the beach of Greek history;
With uncurling of her curls,
History gets curled up fully;
Many Homers, many bards
Go on telling Helen's tale
Go on hailing Helen's hell!
I see pretty Cleopatra
In Anthony's warmer lap
Singing tunes of Roman praise,
Singing what Anthony has,
Singing that Caesar has not!
I see Virgil strolling through
Affluent meadows of Rome
Singing songs from his Aeneid!
I see Sappho of Lesbos
Loosing webs of mind and soul,
Printing on the lips of friends
Verses, now, the world recites!
I see Samson—hairy man—
Laughing in the piano keys
At the crooked Delilah!

I see keys dancing to tunes
Hummed by Voltaire in free France:
In chorus whole Europe sings
Freedom, justice, equity!
I see Simone de Bouva,
Embracing Sartre out of
Love, waltzing across the globe!
I see in *Beautiful Mind*
Nash dancing to mental tunes—
Stronger than what Beethoven
Could hear in his symphonies!

I see myself in all these
Ladies, gentlemen alike,
Feel I am performing some
Stately, lively, mod salsa!
And I think Madame, I sing
With the wings of Time that moves.
I am immortal, Madame,
For these keys, these black, white keys
Sing those everlasting notes,
Which echo across cosmos,
Never to be dead or gone!

Oh, Madame, touch not the keys!
Let the tunes in piano sing,
Let the piano sing in tunes!
Let the tunes in piano dance,
Let the piano dance in tunes!
Touch not piano keys, Madame,
Silence of the piano sings!

Paris, 2008

In Thin, Strained, Coughing, Low Voice

In thin, strained, coughing, low voice
To her man she speaks her woes:
"Weeks have worn on hard, honey!
We're short of necessaries;
We won't eat the next day, sure;
And the next to next day too;
I can't bear the body pain,
Can't bear this terrible cough
And the bouts of high fever;
Now, these constant hunger pangs!"

The coffin-maker hears her
Speak her woes, he knows though; and
Leaves for one steep hill nearby.
Lies ahead a vast ocean,
Whose vastness narrows his soul.
He to himself speaks his woes,
Woes of life— dark, deadly dull!
He thinks he can starve for long,
But what of his poor, weak wife
He can't see crying a bit,
Can't bear her rough, chesty cough,
Can't bear her fever, her pain.
Sobbing in his soul he sits
On the steep hill with no hope,
No duck, no buck, nothing sure.

Night passes with darkness veil;
Owls in boughs blow secret tunes;
Moon stitched to the heavens cries;
Winds blow with the scent of gloom;
Roaring winds whip the shroud off
The frail thin dead body of
The coffin-maker's poor wife.
With a heavy heart he sits

By one side of his courtyard,
Eyes glistening with tears, and soul
Under the load of deep grief.
Just one thought perturbs him much—
"Who would pay for her coffin!?"

Chitral, 2004

Your Eyes are Orators

Your eyes are orators
Of your wondrous beauty

That stays in your mind like
Some prime, artistic thought

Couched in Shakespearian
Expression, form an' style,

That drips from your body
Like Elysian wine,

Which makes Dionysus
Stagger in the heavens,

Makes Muses inspire
Painters, poets to fill

Canvases with warm hues,
Pages with magic words!

Your eyes are not mere eyes:
They're clouds of fire, snow.

Where they look, life looks there;
Where they move, life moves there;

When shut they are like moist
Pearls resting in oysters;

When open, they trigger
A war within a soul.

These pearls are wholly drenched
In life's soft, bold colours.

Two whirlpools of peril,
They sink many a ship

With drowning breakers, waves.
Marlowe's mighty verses

Remain no mightier
Before these charming eyes.

Shakespeare's women pale by
Comparison to just

A coup d'œil of them.
Observing intense beams

Of these jewels, Venus
Claims no supremacy

Over the fetching looks
Which make Cupid bow down.

No Sirens sing better
Than these magical flutes.

Oh Iris, Oh goddess!
Your eyes are orators!

Bristol, 2008

What You Sculpt, I Do Not

What you sculpt, I do not,
    What I carve, you may not,
But hangs still in the mind
    Some careless, clueless rhyme!
We make the same music!

Florence, 2008

Your Leaning Leans me, Pisa

Your leaning leans me, Pisa,
On shoulders of those mortals
Who made you lean on ages!

No wonder you wonder are!
You are a crown of artists!
On Time's lips one tender kiss!
A tune, maestros would wish for!
A verse, Muses would die for!
In moonlight you glint like a
Rose in a goddess's lap:
Her raven tresses on your
Face make chinks for light to glow.
Your leaning is not leaning:
It is a frozen feeling!
Chisel of a real artist
In Time carves better than stone!
Oh, Beauty, you're carved in Time!
You are some knot in Time's rope—
A knot, Trojans would wish for,
To tie Helen with their souls;
A knot Roman Empire
Would wish to tie all states with,
In so solid a fashion
That diadem, which Caesars
Wore, would continue to be
A symbol of elegance.
Oh, great Tower of Pisa!
My people lean like you lean
But their leaning's like rocking!
They're rocking unceasingly.
I wish they cease their rocking,
I wish they lean like you lean!

Pisa, 2008

The Ice Age

the Ice Age
begins anew:

from horizon
to horizon,

volcanoes
are unvoiced

with magma
under rocks pressed;

the rivers, the streams,
the oceans, the cascades, the fountains

are blanketed by snow;
trees, shrubs, boughs

twigs, cones, flowers
are mute on the landscape;

the chilled clouds have
blotted out the solar ball;

every sound a frozen echo,
every light a frosted lamp!

but somewhere
in a valley,

a hill shakes
clearing the ice;

there emerges a word—'NEVER'.

Guildford, Surrey 2007

At a Foot's Distance, Louvre

At a foot's distance, Louvre
Museum behaves like a
Very stern, rude prison guard,
Whose eyes know no courtesy,
Whose face shows no deference!

Like a skylark, my soul flies
Up in the sky restlessly
Tearing wilder winds, singing
Songs of unbridled passion,
To hold in its arms the Moon!

Smashing walls and flinging gate
Only with a single gaze,
Dancing, glowing, dazzling, lo,
Comes out fair Mona Lisa
Throwing round my neck her arms!

I know it's a barter trade!

Paris, 2008

In A Venetian Market

In a Venetian market
At a trendy glass gift shop,
A glass dealer lady in
Quite high-pitched voice forewarns me:

"It's Italy you've blown in!
Dude, in Italian, speak!
Speak no English; got it, eh?
If no, I won't sell you things!"

I smile, glance through her glass shop:
Fine, captivating glass work—
Cut glass vases in all forms,
All colours, shapes an' patterns

One can think of— fills the shop.
Crystal chandeliers or
Hourglasses, all glassware—
Opal, amber, auburn toys,

Mustard, cherry, claret cups,
Lilac, ochre souvenirs,
Shower colours on my mind.
All articles, artefacts

Hoot, jeer, snigger, laugh at me.
Shell pink eyes brimming with tears,
Blood throbbing in her thread veins,
One shiny, coral seabird

Made of finer crystal glass,
In low voice says: 'sorry sir!'
I look in her sad eyes, kiss
Her 'goodbye', eyes moist, smiling!

Venice, 2008

Tears in Her Sapphire Eyes

Tears in her sapphire eyes
   Roll like cobalt blue, rogue waves
On crude shores of Greek islands,
   Blind to laughing inland towns!

Southampton, 2007

Empty like a Trumpet, World

Empty like a trumpet, world
Waits at time's hall for grand songs:
Folk, love, pop; carols, raps, psalms.
He who holds the trumpet's mouth,
Leads the chorus, leads the choir.
O love-bard, grab firm hold of
Trumpet's mouth and fill the space
With dulcet voice, tuneful songs!
Let the time see world afresh!

Xian, 2010

Like Attractive Freckles, Paris

Like attractive
Freckles, Paris

Is sprinkled on
Camus' eyelids!

I sing with treads
The songs of time

Which Camus sang
With me on shores

Of loneliness.
In chorus all

The freckles sing;
His Paris sings!

Echoing Time,
I sing, amble

On his eyelids
Very gently!

His breathing skin
Is touched by feet,

My cold, bare feet,
Which feel the heat

Of ages, times,
Which Camus has

Buried in books,
Buried in Time!

The eye in search
Of Self, of Peace

Of Justice, Love
Of Equity

Is fighting with
Itself for long.

It sees too much,
It feels too much.

The eye sleeps not
Though Camus sleeps!

And I move on
Very gently

To eyelids of
His second eye!

Paris, 2008

The Ink of My Soul

the ink of my soul
replenishes

the pages of Time;
bit by bit the leaves of

this book
get absolutely

doused in ink.
no character,

sign or symbol
stays on any leaf.

each letter, each word
drips from the book

turning it
utterly shriveled.

Islamabad, 2005

My Mind's Both Fag an' Fire

My mind's both fag an' fire.
In a chain I light my nerves
With the lighter of my mind.

My puffs at my mind cover
The air round me with grey smoke.
Lo, my mind coughs everywhere!

Some residents of this town
Pester me with counseling;
They hate mind's persistent cough

And dislike smoke belching out.
They say when smoke curls up, hangs
In the air and chokes breathing,

Say cough's chronic, bad and dry,
Its transmission's threat persists.
But I don't ask for advice!

So, they've launched a fierce campaign
Aimed at proving me a threat.
Their ads, news reach all over;

Anti-smoking processions,
Hygiene slogans an' complaints
Stick at ringing out day, night.

But I just smoke; yeah, just smoke!

Karachi, 2010

Cannot Resist the Mind

Cannot resist the mind!
Cannot resist the feet!
Soul chokes up when blossoms
And cones begin to fall;
And belts out songs when leaves
And twigs begin to sprout.
Moving up, moving down
Magnetizes the feet.

Life in a circle moves,
Justifies itself by
Not derailing from that
Foisted circle line; but
Ceaseless curiosity
Prickles the nerves of mind.

Karachi, 2010

Reality—an Illusion

A stark naked
Black lad, darting

Across the teeth
And the tongue of

The Sahara,
Splatters foot prints

Onto the sand.
Heavens shower

Sweltering heat,
Bake beneath him

Vast sandy ground.
The desert like

Some blistered skin
Simmers under

The flaming sun
In its countless

Searing sand dunes.
Lo, the lad falls,

Never to rise!
Eyes still running:

Illusions are
Reality!

Reality—
An illusion!

Portsmouth, 2007

From the Womb of Beaming Bath

I just dig underneath—
The landscape that has kept

Royal Crescent hanging
To knock at the mind of

A traveler of love—
Unearth the barren Time

That had waited long for
The seed of Jane Austen,

Who rose as a rose from
The soil of grand Sulis,

The womb of beaming Bath!
These natural, pure hot springs

Spout those fresh, novel lines,
Which Novels wish they had,

Novelists wish they wrote!
The Avon keeps fertile

The land, which Jane sowed with
Her gay and merry songs,

Where flowers in chorus
Sing those family songs,

Where beauty's a bit shy,
Where life is ardour, warmth,

Where peace and love reside,
Where heart an' mind are blithe!

Bath, 2007

The Statue of Liberty Now

The Statue of Liberty now
Topples onto the silent earth!

All places of the shaken land
Witness all its splinters fallen.

The Earthen-floor lurches badly
Like Beethoven's fiery track

In rumbling, crashing, booming sounds.
Shrieks, noise all around, but hears none.

Turned deaf, Time complains of dumbness.
The world's turned a dumb Anthony!

London, 2007

At the Southampton Shore

Hazy in the distance
  Plenty of ships in lines
    Seem ardent adherents
      Gathered at Vatican
        For their first admittance!

Southampton, 2008

Under The Scorching Sun

under the scorching sun
with eyelids
beginning to droop,
the leafless boughs
and the arid earth
have been waiting for ages
to fall into
a deep sleep.

Mirpurkhas, 2005

With One Leg Chopped Off

with one leg chopped off,
a half-naked, malnourished, starving child
crawls along
a roasting hot metalled road
utterly oblivious to the
chill and exotic perfume
dancing inside
the luxurious
Aston Martin
screeching across the road.

Kuwait, 2008

Dancing Wildly Her Swift Body

Dancing wildly her swift body
Like cobra creeps through mind's muscles.
Her deft stepping, her rhythmic curves
Inspire Dance Goddess to dance.
Her feet, her hands, her eyes, her legs,
Her breasts, her hips, her thighs, her lips,
Her liveliness, recklessness work
The crowd up into a frenzy.
She turns sheet lightning in the sky
And sets in like incessant rains.
With vacillating breathing, she
Takes rounds an' rounds an' rounds an' rounds;
And freezes on the ground, at last!

Out of joy, buzz, the crowd chucks coins—
Five pence, ten pence, one pound, two pounds.
Then everyone leaves her for more
Fascinating performances
Waiting at the banks of the Thames!

London, 2008

Teensy-Weensy, Tiddly Toys

Tall, rolling hills an' the rain
With biting chill, gusty winds
And the discouraging height
Challenge my feet, pulse an' veins.
People soaked in rain an' snow
Think of no retreat to homes,
Rather chuckling, giggling mount
The saturated course, hills.
In this huge throng of people
One little girl follows me
Hawking, in some breathy tone,
Teensy-weensy, tiddly toys.
I ignore and scale the hill
But in a dolorous mode
The little girl hawks aloud.
I keep on ignoring and
She keeps at hawking her toys.
In a deep tone she complains,
"I've crept on rough stone of life
Lacerating skin and flesh
Of my wretched, luckless soul!
Bro! Am I not worth one buck!?"

Wall of China, Badaling, 2010

Meanings

I
words die
like bubbles,
while meanings
like air
remain inside
the champagne flute!

II
meanings live
like bubbles in a flute,
while words
like air
remain inside
the champagne bottle!

Isle of Wight, 2007

The Goddess of Justice

The Goddess of Justice
Stands on the plinth that shakes.

This impressive statue
Was elegantly hewn

Out of some sacred stone,
Polished by legions of

Angelos, de Vincis,
Placed on the plinth by hosts

Of Christs and Abrahams,
Deified by droves of

Zaroasters and Ramas.
The plinth shakes terribly,

Shakes at the same instant
The statue on the plinth.

Alabaster flakes off
And thick, glossy, old paint

Begins to peel off, lo!
The plinth cleaves into two,

The statue slips over
With its celestial parts

On temporal, dirty
Profane, vile, earthly floor!

Kailash, 2005

A Lonely, Forlorn Hill

a lonely, forlorn hill
in the heart of
an infinite desert
echoes back
the cry of ages.

but the delay
outruns the speed.

Nangarparkar, Thar 2006

A Blank Canvas

A blank canvas
Bitterly cries

Not knowing where
Its tears may drop.

A dead brush on
A corner lies.

Shades, colours in
The doleful hall

Add to glumness,
Add to despair.

The painting of
Cleopatra hangs

In the air as
A question mark!

Woking, Surrey 2008

He Flings a Framed Mirror

He flings a framed mirror
Against a stony wall:

Striking, the mirror falls
Onto the floor, all sides.

He picks up all the shards
And sees that every shard

Makes, plays the same music,
Draws, tints the same image,

Carols the same old song,
Shows the same bleak picture.

"So, why to break the glass?
Why not to break the face?"

Karachi, 2009

The Shepherd Unheard

(Beethoven to a Shepherd)

o Time! may I have
colossal wings and the sinews
of a mythical Albatross
to wing my way above
the volcanic clouds
this shepherd's flute is
sprinkling over my sensitivity?

o flautist! haven't you heard
my violin echo across the globe
with my symphonies
sprinkling seeds of melody
to fertilize the sterile soil of musicality?
deafened, I can spot
my melodies amusing themselves with
Euterpe's crooning locks.
drunk on the wine of my music,
muses trip on the ballroom of history.
see, the Muse of Tragedy
inspires artists to create tunes
of tragedy over my misery!

but not you so inspired be!
your unheard tunes are heavier
than the catastrophes time caused
the Trojans and the Babylonians!
your flute is more resonant
than the one David would play!
my ears may split open at its echo!
your flute, o flautist of tragedy,
thrusts its unheard tunes
into my ears to burst them from within;
like molten copper they burn me to naught!

had it been audible to me what
your flute sings,
I would have been all ears,
would have admired all your labours,
would have been to you what
Aristotle was to Alexander,
would have gifted you what
Prometheus gifted the mankind!

o Time, hear me as I can't hear!
o flautist, spread not
the venom of melody,
hit not my hearing—my Achilles heel!
I wail, I cry, I die!

Rome, 2008

Shifty, Venal, Harlot Minds

Shifty, venal, harlot minds
Fast like stones, pebbles whirl, hit
Their own back, prick their own eyes,
Hit your back too, prick your eyes!
They are like a beggar's bowl.
Who knows who bunged coins in it?

Karachi, 2009

Oh, Majestic Avon!

Oh, majestic Avon!
Identity of bards!

You're not just a river;
You are what chroniclers

Aspire to have as
Colour to beautify

Their crude, rough, dull pages.
Cleaving the breast of Time

You have printed the scent
Of infinity on

The brows of English ship
That sails across the world.

Though narrow, small you are,
There's much in you that has

Drowned travelers of verse,
Of fancy, love in your

Cheery, drunken waves to
Make them one with the soil,

Where Bard of Avon lived,
Where pearls of a golden

History are buried in
A splendid, royal style.

Paying homage to your
August water, I leave

To return home to cast
My bigger half into

The deep river Indus!

Stratford-upon-Avon, 2008

Not Flabbergasted, Rocked

Not flabbergasted, rocked,
I catch what's in the night:

The Big Ben clock thaws melts
With hour and minute

Hands turning huge serpents,
Which hiss an' hiss an' hiss,

Can sting bite if approached.
Sizes, shapes an' patterns

Of numbers have altered—
1 has turned a tower

About to smash into
The Tower of London;

3 has turned a black tomb
Shattering into shards

On Westminster Abbey.
The clock has shaped itself

Into an old woman
Whose lifeless hair flow down

Over the North, the South,
Over the East, the West.

The Bell chimes ceaselessly
Blowing shrill, piercing sounds

Across the Parliament,
The Buckingham Palace,

The Victoria Gate,
Beyond the river Thames!

London, 2007

Dreams Hopes Burn

her parched lips,
ever-spiritless eyes,
pasty, sallow skin
strip
the brightly coloured paint
off the celebrated human saga;
she breathes but...
    dreams hopes burn
    in the perpetual
    graveyard
    of her flesh!

an imitation of imitation,
she has got no place
in Utopia;
faltering, she climbs up
the Empyrean
from ever-burning Inferno
but as usual
tumbles down into
the same abyss!
    dreams hopes burn
    in the perpetual
    graveyard
    of her flesh!

one can see Time
drowning her in the waters
of carnal ugliness
the nature has bestowed upon her.
one can see Time reveling in
her helplessness
when wolves
pull her emotions apart
by pressing her soul

against the wall of
sensuality!
    dreams hopes burn
    in the perpetual
    graveyard
    of her flesh!

Jamshoro, 2009

A Torso of a Mind

a torso of a mind
has been planted
on the head of people.

echo, only echo
reverberates
through the land.

Bhit Shah, 2009

Hemlock

Socrates
    killed
        hemlock!

Athens, 2008

The Drama

the drama,
like the snowflakes in the wind,
has strewn the North, the South,
the East, the West.

someone has shuffled
its letters and words
and sprinkled them
onto this land.

having drained away with water,
the punctuation marks
(except the question
and the exclamation marks

which are seen swirling around the islands)
silt up
the delta.
the dialogues

have gone missing
somewhere in the metropolis,
and exactly where
the inverted commas are,

one is not sure about.
some of the scenes
have occupied plateaus,
the hilly areas,

and most of them
have crumbled
into many parts;
hence, visible

almost everywhere.
which part joins which,
is nothing but
a puzzle!

most of the characters
have entered huts
and the rest burst into
chateaus and castles.

no one can draw a distinction
between common and
proper nouns.
the whole grammar

has turned a
disarranged matrix.
a team of
Shylocks and Machiavellis

is busy writing
a new drama!

Guildford, Surrey 2007

At Twilight—I

at twilight
the ship has sailed
off the shore

leaving
flotsam and jetsam
behind

to float in the waves.
some kids
at the shore

amuse themselves with
the distant echo of the ship;
others have plunged into

the water
with part conscious,
part subconscious hope

to come by something
still nifty, neat, of use from amongst
the odds and sods, the leftovers.

parents are yelling at them
to stop romping around
as the dusk has approached

and soon
the night will close in.
though no more is

the ship visible,
no longer its echo heard now,
the kids

against their parents' call
are having fun
till they wear themselves out.

Keti Bandur, 2006

At Twilight—II

at twilight
the ship has sailed
off the shore

leaving flotsam and jetsam behind
to float in the waves.
kids at the shore are

riveted by the echo of the ship;
their return to their homes
is eagerly awaited

as the dusk has settled
and soon
the darkness will descend,

but the echo of the ship
halts their movement.
they sit together

and reflect.
after quite a while,
wreathing with ecstasy,

all of them move
in different directions
off the sea.

the darkness has kissed
every corner of the locale,
the lamp of the moon

is not lit in the sky,
and the kids have
clustered together again at the shore

with teeny-weeny lamps,
eyes sparkling with
ethereal light.

though not with expertise,
their little hands work on woods
very imaginatively.

Keti Bandur, 2006

The Trumpets Blow

The trumpets blow;
Locale echoes
With wedding songs.

The bride and groom
Are just blissed out.
The parents, friends,
The neighbours and
The guests go mad
Dancing wildly!
The waiters go
Round pouring beer,
Red wine, white wine,
Rosé, champagne.
The wine glasses
Get topped up as
Soon as emptied.
The vibrant songs
Ooze an aura
Of mirth and fun.
Life sings dances
In souls; and death

Just smirks unseen!

Tianjin, China 2010

Birth

birth,
yeah, birth,
like a serpent
slithers through the rolling plains
and craggy coastlines of
your mind and soul
to bite here and there,
everywhere!

you are dying
to be born!

St. Fagan's, Cardiff 2008

Thirst, Thirst, Thirst, Eternal Thirst

Thirst, thirst, thirst, eternal thirst
Bumped off Tamburlaine, the Khans,

Hitlers, Neros, tyrants, kings!
Endless Adam's ale on tap

To these thirsty Adamites
Pointless and untouchable.

History poured elixir but
Could not sate their raging thirst—

Thirst, thirst, their eternal thirst!
Now Time is thirstier than

Could be Gog and Magog; An'
To slake its insatiable

Thirst, there's water but useless
There is tasty blood but less.

Amsterdam, 2008

Scavengers

Scavengers—oh, dead eaters,
Land in swarms, attack corpses!
Burnish all your tools, weapons:
Crunching, munching, chomping teeth,
Perforating, piercing tongues,
Peeling paws an' spear-like nails,
Drilling beaks an' scaring eyes!
Corpses in piles on the earth
Swell an' spread, fast multiply:
Some corpses in mainland lie,
Some in water, some on hills;
Some bloated, bloodied, burnt, torn,
Poisoned, rotten, mangled, drowned!
Yachts of time—days, decades—cruise
And the scene is on and on!

Grow corpses, rapidly grow!
You have good fortune, you are
Dead in souls, in bodies live!
No chagrin, anguish an' pain.
Safe from torments mind inflicts
On moments of existence.
No harm if your bodies are
Chewed by hungry, greedy teeth!

Scavengers—oh, dead eaters,
Land in swarms, attack corpses,
Bite them, eat them bit by bit!
They won't yell, won't wail, won't whine!

Lahore, 2005

Bruno is Burnt at the Stake

Bruno is burnt at the stake:
Fangs of fire rip apart

Brain, rupture its nerves except
His fancy that has taken,

In the veins of Time, refuge.
Bleeding profusely air sobs,

Drinks blazing poison the earth,
But the scorching heat dies not.

To the bystanders on ground
Just fire an' flame's the scene.

Who have him burnt, they know not!
They know not the burnt, alas!

Fire's not the only play!

Islamabad, 2005

Catch Tropical Winds

catch tropical winds,
uproot the cacti of ink

you've sown
the soil of Time's pages with.

spines breathing in these plants
wound the eyes which touch them.

scarlet letters, scarlet words,
turned Macbeth's dagger,

rend the lips of Time.
have you ever feasted your eyes on

a day when the sun beats down on
the fields of sunflower?

if *No,* meet Van Gogh!
oh, chronicler!

let Egypt suffer
the obliteration

of history ramparts.
let Kabul writhe on

the bumpy, rutted path
of her politics.

let Sparta delight in the training of
their nude athletes.

and hark! Socrates
is going to get

his death sentence for
leading the Athenian youth astray.

the private chamber
of the priest-king of

Moen-Jo-Daro
echoes with

the quick, nimble stepping
of the Dancing Girl.

oh, chronicler! do turn
a sculptor.

catch hold of a chisel,
remove the dust from

the Statue of Time.
history will appear

in an unbroken frame
with an undamaged face!

Cardiff, Wales 2008

Time Melts

time melts
in your blood-red eyes
as hope melts
in the currents of
the River Styx.

the harbingers of
a turbulent storm,
your eyes forewarn of
an untold deluge.

forget not a whit!
let no letter and word melt!
freeze all colons,
commas, phrases...
extinguish the sun
that appears on your eyelashes!

you are to this land
no better than Cassandra!

Hyderabad, 2009

In the Venetian Water

in the Venetian Water
at sunset
Gondolas
seem like
ants
marching
to and from
their nests.

Venice, 2008

Every Face

Old or young,
Every face—
An idol!

And the world
Temple—vast,
Gigantic!

How puzzling
It's to find
Men in gods!

Vatican City, 2008

Insensate Violin

oh, insensate violin!
the violinist
will lift his bow

and make the surrounding air
resonate
with tunes.

the tunes will flow
from your strings
as arrows shoot from a bow.

air wounded, will drop
as melody
to ensconce herself

in every corner.
all will be dancing:
the hosts, the guests,

the player, the listeners,
the curtains, the doors,
the champagne flutes,

except a broken heart
that will gradually turn
a sea of

melting ice.
oh, numb creature!
turn thy strings

into magic waves
and fall into
a bottomless black hole!

never be heard,
never be found.

Florence, 2008

Sing to Me no More, Sirens!

Sing to me no more, Sirens!
Sing to them no more, Sirens!

Lay laurel wreaths on the harp
You keep on playing, but the

Labyrinths you fashion for
Wreaking havoc on people

Are no better than mummies.
Here reigns no Menelaus

Who is bested, mastered by
Fleshly beauty of Helen.

Here lives Prometheus who
Pours fire into men's souls.

Unhitching your occult nets,
See, how these sailors sail off...

Unafraid of sea monsters,
Not vexed by sea Sphinx riddles,

Not attracted by Helens,
Part winds, part wings move away...

Sing to them no more, Sirens!
Sing to me no more, Sirens!

Amsterdam, 2008

A Sea

a sea
of skin-less bodies
navigated by serrated knives

is painted deep crimson
by spear-haired
brushes!

an ocean
of body-less skins
sailed by

dagger-made ships
is sketched
on the canvas

by razor-sharp
fingers!
a giant art gallery

of flesh and blood
gleams
in the pupils!

Florence, 2008

Alabaster Statue

o, alabaster statue!
you wear
peace
from head to toe.
some cold pale light
radiates from you
that quite cosmetically
pastes brightness
into the skin of
my soul
leaving its flesh
and bones
un-kissed!

Vatican City, 2008

The Dotted Line

as a child
I scrawl
your name
on a dotted line of Time.

the pencil strays
off the line,
sometimes above,
at times below.

I erase and re-write,
re-erase and write again
but your name
remains

half-written.
and now
I find the dotted line
about to be erased.

Mirpurkhas, 2006

The Painting

The painting of
New World Order
Melts on canvas:
Shades, hues, colours,
Lines, all detached
From dots, from curves,
From each other;
The browns westwards,
The blues eastwards,
The black northwards,
The white southwards.
Awkward mixture!
All wanting in
Definition.
The lines, the curves,
Shades, hues, colours,
All panicky,
All upsetting.
The painter is
Weirdly shocked.
He picks his brush
An' looks around
To find some hue
Some shade, colour
From tins but all
The tins empty
In corners smile.

London, 2008

Put out the Sun

put out the sun
and hurl it
beyond
the edge
of the cosmos
to partner me!
let it dwell there
as a mark of
civilization!

Hyderabad, 2006

www.ingramcontent.com/pod-product-compliance
Ingram Content Group UK Ltd.
Pitfield, Milton Keynes, MK11 3LW, UK
UKHW040019200726
13854UKWH00001B/265

9 781456 773854